Cat Dental Care 101

A GUIDE TO HEALTHY CAT TEETH

ISBN-978-1-0670394-0-0

CAROLE MALONE
OWNER - WHISKERS & PAWS LUXURY CAT RESORT

There's a saying that we don't choose cats—they choose us. In my case, they didn't just choose me; they shaped my entire life's journey. From those early childhood days when our family home was warmed by the presence of our feline companions, to now running one of New Zealand's premier luxury cat resorts, cats have been the constant thread weaving through my story.

My path in the world of cat care began as a volunteer at the SPCA, where every shift deepened my understanding of these magnificent creatures. Soon, I found myself fostering kittens, experiencing both the joy and challenge of preparing them for their forever homes. But sometimes, as any foster parent knows, the heart has other plans. That's how Smokey and Bandit, two of my foster kittens, became permanent members of our family, joining our seasoned seniors, Ocean and Chloe.

This love for cats eventually led to an ambitious dream: creating a purpose-built luxury cat resort in our apple orchard in Hawkes Bay, New Zealand.

WWW.WHISKERSANDPAWS.CO.NZ

WHISKERS & PAWS - THE LUXURY CAT RESORT

After two years of careful planning, navigating consents, and overseeing construction, Whiskers & Paws Luxury Cat Resort opened it's doors in October 2016.

While life threw us some curveballs—including my mother's Alzheimer's diagnosis, which changed our original plans for running the resort together—we persevered.

Today, over nine years later, our resort has become a trusted haven for more than 2,300 regular clients, where we care for up to 70 cats daily.

The success of our resort and the continuous questions from cat owners inspired me to create a series of self-help books. My goal is simple: to share the knowledge I've gathered over years of professional cat care, helping you to provide the best possible life for your feline family members.

For daily doses of feline joy and a peek into life at our resort, I invite you to follow us on Facebook, where we share updates about our current guests and their adventures.

Facebook-whiskersandpawsluxurycatresort

WWW.WHISKERSANDPAWS.CO.NZ

WHISKERS & PAWS CAT BOOK SERIES

In these pages, you'll find practical advice, proven techniques, and heartfelt insights drawn from both my personal experience and professional expertise. Whether you're a new cat parent or have shared your life with cats for years, I hope you'll find valuable information to enhance your journey together.

Welcome aboard the journey to ensuring your fluffy companion enjoys a life filled with joy, health, and gleaming smiles!

Picture this: your cat, with vibrant, healthy teeth, experiencing every day to the fullest without a hint of discomfort. It might sound like a dream, but with your commitment and a dash of love, this can become your reality. In this opening chapter, we delve deep into the heart of why dental care is so integral for your feline friend. This isn't just about avoiding bad breath, it's about preventing a cascade of health issues that can dampen your cat's spirit and shorten its lifespan. By understanding the value of dental health, you're taking a crucial step towards ensuring your cat leads a long, blissful life.

WHY FELINE DENTAL CARE MATTERS

This book focuses on the importance of cat dental care. It begins with the general health benefits, moving to the potential risks of neglect, and ending with the impact on the cat's overall wellness.

CONTENTS

1. INTRODUCTION TO FELINE DENTAL CARE

2. UNDERSTANDING A CAT'S DENTAL ANATOMY

3. SIGNS OF DENTAL PROBLEMS IN CATS

4. ROUTINE CAT DENTAL CHECK-UPS

5. AT-HOME DENTAL CARE TECHNIQUES

6. CHOOSING THE RIGHT DENTAL CARE PRODUCTS

7. THE ROLE OF DIET IN DENTAL HEALTH

8. UNDERSTANDING CAT DENTAL PROCEDURESCT

9. PREVENTING DENTAL PROBLEMS

10. THE IMPACT OF DENTAL HEALTH ON OVERALL WELLNESS

11. CONCLUSION: CARING FOR YOUR CAT'S TEETH: A LIFELONG COMMITMENT

DISCLAIMER

The information provided in this book is intended for general informational purposes only. While every effort has been made to ensure accuracy, I am not a veterinarian or a qualified veterinary nurse. This book is not a substitute for professional veterinary advice, diagnosis, or treatment. If you have specific questions or concerns about your cat's health, behavior, or well-being, please consult a licensed veterinarian or a qualified veterinary professional. I cannot assume responsibility for any consequences resulting from the use of information contained in this book.

CHAPTER 1

INTRODUCTION TO FELINE DENTAL CARE

WWW.WHISKERSANDPAWS.CO.NZ

INTRODUCTION

Why should we zoom in on our cat's dental health, you might wonder?
The reason is both simple and profound.
A cat's oral health is a reflection of their overall well-being. Neglecting it can lead to a host of painful, expensive problems down the line. Yet, fear not! We're here to walk you through transforming dental care from a chore into a bonding activity that both you and your cat will grow to enjoy. We're set to uncover the myriad benefits of robust dental care, highlight the dangers of neglect, and, most importantly, showcase how a healthy mouth lays the foundation for a vibrant, active life for your furry family member.

Imagine the difference it makes when your cat isn't plagued by oral discomfort. They can relish their favorite treats, frolic around with their toys, and share more cuddle times, all because of the absence of pain. That's the power of proper dental care. It's more than just brushing teeth; it's about enriching your cat's life in every possible way.

GENERAL HEALTH BENEFITS

Diving into the world of feline dental care, let's start with the stark reality: most cats begin to show signs of periodontal disease by the age of three. This ailment, beginning with seemingly harmless plaque, can quickly escalate into tartar build-up, leading to swollen gums, infections, and, in severe cases, tooth loss. The good news, however, is that this progression is not inevitable. Regular dental care, through brushing and professional check-ups, can halt disease in its tracks, ensuring your cat's mouth remains a fortress of health.

But why stop at the mouth? Bacterial infections originating from dental disease can hitch a ride through the bloodstream, setting their sights on your cat's heart, liver, and kidneys. The consequences can be dire, affecting not just their oral health but their overall vitality. This is where the importance of professional cleanings and home care intertwine, forming a shield that protects your cat's entire body from the microscopic invaders that threaten their well-being.

A happy cat is an active cat-one who can enjoy every aspect of life without the shadow of discomfort looming over. Good dental health gifts your cat the freedom to enjoy their meals, engage in playtime, and socialize without the hindrance of oral pain. It's about nurturing a lifestyle where your cat can thrive, expressing their unique personality to the fullest.

RISKS ASSOCIATED WITH NEGLECT

The path of dental neglect is fraught with dangers. Tooth loss and severe infections are just the tip of the iceberg. These dental woes can lead to a domino effect, where one problem escalates into another, creating a cycle of pain and discomfort for your beloved pet. Awareness and timely action are your best defenses against these outcomes. By staying vigilant for signs of dental distress and embracing preventive care, you can safeguard your cat from the pitfalls of neglect.

Cats are notoriously stoic creatures, often concealing their pain until it becomes unbearable. This means that by the time you notice something's amiss, they might have been suffering in silence for far too long. Regular dental check-ups serve as a critical tool in uncovering hidden issues, ensuring your cat doesn't endure unnecessary pain. It's about being proactive, catching problems before they escalate into major health concerns.

Poor dental health is a gateway to systemic health issues. The implications of neglected dental care extend far beyond the mouth, potentially compromising your cat's systemic health. Effective dental care transcends simple tooth brushing; it involves a holistic approach to health, integrating diet, lifestyle, and regular veterinary consultations into a comprehensive wellness plan.

IMPACT ON OVERALL WELLNESS

Nutrition plays a pivotal role in your cat's life, and healthy teeth are essential for them to eat properly and absorb nutrients. Compromised dental health can make mealtime a painful ordeal, leading to malnutrition and a host of related health issues. Selecting the right diet, enriched with nutrients that support dental health, can make a world of difference. It's about providing a balanced, nourishing meal plan that caters not just to your cat's taste buds but to their dental and overall health as well.

Behavior is a window into your cat's well-being. Dental pain can manifest in changes in demeanor, from aggression to withdrawal. Understanding these cues is crucial in identifying and addressing dental issues before they escalate. By maintaining a vigilant eye and fostering a stress-free environment, you can help mitigate the behavioral impacts of dental discomfort, ensuring your cat remains sociable, playful, and loving.

Ultimately, the pursuit of good dental health is a journey towards extending your cat's lifespan. A commitment to regular dental care is a commitment to more years of companionship, adventure, and love. Through proactive care, you're not just ensuring your cat's smile remains bright; you're opening the doors to a future filled with health, happiness, and boundless joy.

By reaching the end of this introduction, you've taken a significant step towards understanding the profound importance of dental care in your cat's life. We celebrate your willingness to embark on this journey, recognizing the impactful difference your actions will make. Your dedication to your cat's dental health is a testament to the depth of your love and commitment. Together, let's stride towards a future where every purr is a testament to a life well-lived, and every smile is a beacon of health. Here's to embarking on this path of dental wellness, ensuring years of happiness and health for your feline friend. Thank you for your dedication, and may your journey be filled with many rewarding moments and healthy smiles.

The journey into the world of feline dental care is much like embarking on a grand adventure with your feline companion by your side. It's an exploration into the unknown, filled with opportunities for growth, learning, and deepening the bond between you and your pet. As we delve deeper into the significance of maintaining stellar dental hygiene for your cat, we'll uncover strategies, tips, and heartwarming stories that highlight the transformative power of proper dental care.

Commencing this voyage, it's essential to acknowledge the silent epidemic that plagues the world of our whiskered friends. Dental disease, often overlooked and underestimated, is a formidable foe that, if left unchecked, can stealthily undermine the health and happiness of our beloved pets. This chapter serves as your map and compass, guiding you through the terrain of dental care, illuminating paths to prevent disease, and empowering you with the knowledge to protect your cat's health.

As we navigate through the intricacies of dental care, it's crucial to remember the profound impact our actions have on the lives of our cats. Every brushing session, every dental check-up, every informed choice we make contributes to a tapestry of wellness that not only enhances the quality of life for our furry companions but also strengthens the unbreakable bond we share with them. This journey is one of mutual respect, understanding, and love-a testament to the incredible role we play in the lives of our pets.

In the chapters that follow, we will explore the cornerstones of effective feline dental care, from the basics of brushing to the intricacies of dietary choices. We'll dispel myths, tackle common challenges, and celebrate the victories, both big and small, that come from dedicated care. Each section is designed to equip you with the tools and confidence needed to navigate the world of feline dental health, ensuring that your cat can enjoy a life of joy, vitality, and sparkling smiles.

Embrace this journey with an open heart and mind, ready to learn, adapt, and grow alongside your feline friend. Together, you'll discover the joys of healthy living, the satisfaction of overcoming obstacles, and the unparalleled happiness that comes from a life well-lived. Welcome to the world of feline dental care-a world where love, health, and whisker-tickling smiles abound.

"A cat's smile may be subtle, but their teeth tell the whole story of health, hunting, and heart. Cherish those tiny fangs—they're as much a part of their charm as their purrs."

CHAPTER 2

UNDERSTANDING A CAT'S DENTAL ANATOMY

WWW.WHISKERSANDPAWS.CO.NZ

INTRODUCTION

Welcome to what may be one of the most enlightening chapters in your journey through cat ownership! Venturing into the world of your cat's dental care might seem overwhelming at first glance, but rest assured, demystifying the intricate details of your furry friend's dental anatomy is not only intriguing but paramount to their well-being. By the time we reach the end of this chapter, the thought of exploring your cat's oral cavity will spark more excitement than apprehension. So, let's set off on this educational expedition together. With a bit of knowledge and understanding, you're about to become a pivotal player in ensuring your cat's pearly whites stay healthy and strong.

Starts with a basic description of cat dental anatomy, progresses to the unique aspects of feline teeth, and concludes with common dental problems in cats.

THE BASICS OF CAT DENTAL ANATOMY

Embarking on our journey, it's essential to start with the foundation - the basics of cat dental anatomy. Did you know that an adult cat boasts a collection of 30 teeth? Meanwhile, those heart-meltingly cute kittens are born without any visible teeth, developing a temporary set of baby teeth that start to emerge around the two-week mark. By six months, these deciduous teeth give way to their permanent successors, marking a significant milestone in a kitten's development.

Cats are armed with a variety of teeth types, each serving its unique purpose. They possess incisors, which are small and sharp for detailed nibbling; canines, which are long and pointed for tearing food; premolars, and molars, which are designed for grinding down their meals. This diverse array of teeth is a testament to their carnivorous heritage, requiring a dental structure capable of processing a diet rich in meat.

Diving deeper into the anatomy of a cat's mouth reveals more than just their teeth. Cats have a powerful jaw, but unlike ours, their jaw movement is limited to an up-and-down motion. This lack of side-to-side movement is perfectly adapted to their dietary needs, focusing on the efficient consumption of meat.

UNIQUE ASPECTS OF FELINE TEETH

As we delve further, the unique aspects of feline dental anatomy come to light. The sharpness of a cat's canine teeth is remarkable, designed to grip and tear through their prey with precision. Imagine the efficiency of these natural tools as your cat engages with their favorite toy, mimicking the act of capturing prey. Additionally, nestled within the back of the mouth lies the carnassial tooth, a formidable element crucial for shearing flesh. This specialized tooth operates much like a pair of scissors, seamlessly cutting through meat.

When comparing feline dental anatomy to that of humans, the contrast is stark. Our omnivorous diet necessitates a different dental structure, equipped with teeth suitable for grinding a variety of foods, including vegetables and grains. In contrast, cats' teeth are streamlined for a predominantly carnivorous diet, emphasizing the sharpness and tearing ability over grinding surfaces.

It's fascinating to consider how evolution has shaped the mouths of these incredible animals to suit their dietary needs perfectly. The efficiency with which they can consume their food speaks volumes about the importance of understanding these anatomical features. Knowing the purpose behind each type of tooth can help cat owners appreciate the natural behaviors and dietary preferences of their feline companions.

COMMON DENTAL PROBLEMS IN CATS

Transitioning from the marvels of feline dental structure, it's imperative to address the less pleasant, yet equally important topic of dental issues in cats. Periodontal disease tops the list, beginning innocently as plaque buildup but potentially escalating to severe health complications if left unchecked. Another distressing condition is tooth resorption, where a tooth gradually deteriorates and is absorbed back into the body, often leading to significant discomfort for the affected cat. Additionally, feline stomatitis and halitosis (bad breath) serve as indicators of potential dental problems, necessitating prompt attention. Equally concerning are Feline Odontoclastic Resorptive Lesions (FORLs), a condition that can cause immense pain and requires immediate veterinary intervention.

Fortunately, many dental afflictions can be averted with diligent care and preventative measures. Regular veterinary checkups stand as the cornerstone of early problem detection, enabling interventions before conditions worsen. Moreover, at-home dental care, including tooth brushing, may seem daunting but can evolve into a rewarding ritual that strengthens the bond between you and your cat. The role of diet in dental health cannot be overstated, with certain foods promoting dental wellness more effectively than others. Incorporating dental toys and treats into your cat's routine can also play a pivotal role in maintaining oral hygiene, offering a fun yet functional way to keep their teeth clean.

CONCLUSION

By now, you should feel empowered with the knowledge to make a profound difference in your cat's dental health. Understanding the intricacies of your cat's dental anatomy and being aware of the common issues that can arise are crucial steps toward ensuring they lead a happy, healthy life. Your commitment to your cat's well-being is commendable, and with the insights gained from this chapter, you're well-equipped to tackle any dental challenges that may come your way. Here's to embarking on a journey filled with healthy teeth and joyous purrs, celebrating each step you take towards preserving your cat's dental health.

"A cat's teeth may be small, but they hold stories of evolution, instinct, and survival. They are reminders that within every gentle housecat lives the heart of a fierce hunter."

CHAPTER 3

SIGNS OF DENTAL PROBLEMS IN CATS

WWW.WHISKERSANDPAWS.CO.NZ

INTRODUCTION

Welcome, dear cat enthusiasts, to a critical chapter in our shared journey to ensure the health and happiness of our beloved feline companions-focusing on their dental care. When it comes to our cats, we often focus on their diet, exercise, and cuddles, but their dental health can sometimes be overlooked. Yet, it's as crucial as any other aspect of their care. Ignoring a cat's dental health can lead to issues that affect not just their mouth, but their overall well-being and quality of life. Fortunately, you're about to embark on a path that will turn you into a vigilant guardian of your cat's dental health. By the end of this chapter, you'll be well-versed in spotting the early signs of dental trouble, understanding the progression of dental diseases, and knowing when it's time to seek professional help. Let's dive into the fascinating world of cat dental care, shall we?

Begins by identifying early signs of dental problems, then explains the progression of these signs, and ends with advice on when to seek veterinary help.

IDENTIFYING EARLY SIGNS OF DENTAL PROBLEMS IN CATS

The journey to ensuring your cat's dental health starts with recognizing the early signs of trouble. Imagine your cat's mouth as a hidden world that you're about to explore. The first signpost in this world is bad breath. While it's tempting to dismiss bad breath as a result of your cat's latest meal, it's often a red flag for underlying dental problems. A healthy cat's breath shouldn't send you recoiling; if it does, it's time to pay attention.

Moving deeper into this hidden world, you might notice changes in your cat's eating habits. Perhaps they're not as excited about mealtime as they once were, or maybe they're dropping food out of their mouth or chewing only on one side. These are not mere quirks; they're signals of discomfort or pain in their mouth.

Cats are masters of disguise, especially when it comes to pain. However, they do offer clues. A cat pawing at its mouth or rubbing its face more than usual is attempting to tell you something isn't right. These behaviors are their way of coping with discomfort.

Direct signs like gum and tooth anomalies are more straightforward indicators of dental distress. Healthy gums should be pink, not red or swollen, and teeth should be clean, without any brownish tartar buildup. Loose teeth are a definite cry for help.

Other signs might be less direct but equally telling. Excessive drooling, for instance, or a sudden reluctance to be petted around the face area can also point to dental discomfort. These symptoms, while less common, are crucial pieces of the puzzle.

UNDERSTANDING THE PROGRESSION OF DENTAL PROBLEMS

Dental problems in cats don't just appear out of nowhere; they follow a progression that, if interrupted early, can prevent a lot of pain and health issues down the line. Plaque, a sticky layer of food debris and bacteria, is where it all begins. If not removed, plaque hardens into tartar, setting the stage for gingivitis, an inflammation of the gums that spells trouble.

Gingivitis is like a red flag waving, signaling that tartar is winning the battle against your cat's dental health. Left unchecked, this condition escalates to periodontitis, a serious infection that attacks the deeper structures supporting the teeth. At this stage, tooth loss is a real possibility, along with the risk of the infection spreading into the bloodstream and reaching vital organs.

It's a common misconception that dental health only affects the mouth. The truth is, the impact of dental diseases can ripple through the entire body. The bacteria from the mouth can enter the bloodstream, potentially harming the heart, liver, and kidneys. It's a stark reminder that taking care of your cat's teeth is taking care of their entire body.

WHEN TO SEEK VETERINARY HELP

Knowing when to seek veterinary help is crucial in managing your cat's dental health. Any signs of dental distress we've discussed warrant a trip to the vet. Regular dental check-ups, at least once a year, should be a non-negotiable part of your cat's health care routine. These visits are the cornerstone of prevention, allowing for early detection and intervention.

Preparing for a vet visit involves more than just making an appointment. Observe your cat closely in the days leading up to the visit. Note any changes in behavior, eating habits, or any of the specific signs of dental distress you've learned about. This information is invaluable to your vet and can significantly aid in diagnosing and treating any issues.

Treatment options your vet might recommend can vary widely, from professional cleanings to address plaque and tartar buildup, to more serious interventions like extractions in the case of advanced periodontal disease. Understanding these options, asking questions, and being involved in the decision-making process can make the experience less stressful for both you and your cat.

Prevention is the most powerful tool in your arsenal against dental disease. Regular tooth brushing using cat-specific toothpaste, providing dental-friendly toys and treats, and feeding a diet that promotes dental health are all proactive steps you can take. By adopting a comprehensive approach to dental care, you're not just preventing dental problems; you're ensuring a happier, healthier life for your feline friend.

CONCLUSION

Embarking on this journey to protect and maintain your cat's dental health is a testament to your dedication and love for your feline companion. It's a path that requires vigilance, commitment, and a proactive approach, but the rewards-a happy, healthy cat with a bright smile-are immeasurable. Remember, your efforts today lay the foundation for your cat's well-being tomorrow. So, let's raise a glass (or in this case, a toothbrush) to a future of healthy teeth and bright smiles for our beloved cats. Thank you for being an essential part of this journey. Your commitment to your cat's health is a powerful force for good, and together, we can make a significant difference in their lives. Here's to many more years of joyful purrs and healthy grins!

"In every playful bite and tender groom lies the essence of a cat. Their teeth are more than tools; they're a testament to their wild ancestry and gentle spirit alike."

CHAPTER 4

ROUTINE CAT DENTAL CHECK-UPS

WWW.WHISKERSANDPAWS.CO.NZ

INTRODUCTION

Opens with the importance of regular check-ups, continues with what to expect during these visits, and concludes with tips on finding a good veterinary dentist.

Welcome to the comprehensive guide dedicated to one of the most crucial, yet often overlooked, aspects of feline care: dental health. If you've picked up this guide, you're already stepping in the right direction towards ensuring your beloved cat enjoys a life of well-being, free from dental discomfort. It's a well-known fact that cats are incredibly stoic creatures, often masking pain or discomfort with an almost infuriating finesse. This characteristic, while admirable, places the onus on us, their caretakers, to remain vigilant and proactive regarding their health needs, dental care being paramount among these.

THE IMPORTANCE OF REGULAR DENTAL CHECK-UPS

The journey towards optimal dental health for your cat begins with a commitment to regular dental check-ups. These visits serve as a critical line of defense against the onset of dental diseases, which, if left unchecked, can escalate into serious health complications. Early detection plays a pivotal role here, akin to a detective uncovering clues before a situation worsens. Diseases such as gingivitis and periodontitis are not just mere inconveniences; they are harbingers of potential agony and can significantly impair your cat's quality of life if they progress too far.

Imagine, if you will, the domino effect of untreated dental issues: beginning with the obvious discomfort in the mouth, escalating to difficulties in eating, and culminating in the potential development of life-threatening conditions affecting vital organs like the heart and kidneys. It's a grim picture, but not an inevitable one. Regular dental check-ups can dramatically alter this trajectory, ensuring that your cat's teeth remain in pristine condition, thereby safeguarding its overall health and happiness.

Understanding the stakes involved helps to highlight the significant role that these dental check-ups play in your cat's life. It's not merely about preventing bad breath or dental discomfort; it's about affirming a commitment to your cat's overall well-being. Ensuring that you keep these appointments is an act of love, reflecting your desire to see your cat thrive.

WHAT TO EXPECT DURING A DENTAL CHECK-UP

Understanding what a dental check-up entails can demystify the process, making it less daunting for both you and your cat. The visit typically starts with a visual inspection, where the vet looks for signs of plaque and tartar build-up, inflammation, and any other abnormalities that might indicate dental disease. Special tools may be employed to examine the teeth and gums thoroughly, ensuring no stone is left unturned, so to speak.

Following this, dental X-rays might be taken to provide a glimpse beneath the gum line, offering invaluable insights into the health of the tooth roots and the jawbone. This step is crucial, as many dental issues originate where the eye cannot see. The cleaning process follows, involving scaling to remove plaque and tartar and polishing to smooth the tooth surfaces. This is usually done under anesthesia to ensure the comfort and safety of your feline friend.

The introduction of anesthesia into the cleaning process is a critical measure that addresses the unique challenges of providing dental care to cats. It ensures that the procedure is stress-free and painless, allowing for a thorough cleaning that would otherwise be impossible. The vet's ability to work without the cat moving ensures a level of detail and care that significantly contributes to the overall success of the visit.

Post-examination, the vet will likely share personalized advice for home dental care. This could range from brushing techniques to recommendations for dental health products tailored to your cat's specific needs. The goal is to arm you with the knowledge and tools necessary to continue the good work at home, keeping your cat's teeth clean and healthy between visits.

TIPS FOR FINDING A GOOD VETERINARY DENTIST

Securing the services of a qualified and compassionate veterinary dentist is akin to discovering a hidden gem. Certifications and qualifications should be your initial filters in this quest, as these credentials are indicative of a vet's commitment to and proficiency in dental care. Recommendations from trusted sources, such as friends, family, or your primary vet, can be invaluable in this search, providing you with firsthand accounts of their experiences.

Online reviews also serve as a modern-day compass, guiding you through the experiences of others to help you make an informed decision. However, the true test comes during the consultation. This is your opportunity to assess everything from the vet's communication skills to their interaction with your cat and the overall ambiance of the clinic. A good veterinary dentist will make you feel heard, respected, and confident in the care your cat will receive.

The consultation is your chance to ask questions and express any concerns you might have. It's also an opportunity to observe how the vet interacts with your cat. A vet who takes the time to gently acclimate your cat to the new environment, showing patience and understanding, is someone who genuinely cares about the well-being of their feline patients.

MAINTAINING GOOD DENTAL HEALTH BETWEEN CHECK-UPS

The responsibility of maintaining your cat's dental health extends beyond the vet's office. Daily brushing, while perhaps challenging at first, is the cornerstone of home dental care. Investing the time to acclimate your cat to this routine can pay dividends in their dental health. The right tools, including a cat-specific toothbrush and toothpaste, can make this task more manageable and even enjoyable for your cat.

Diet also plays a crucial role in dental health, with certain foods formulated to reduce plaque and tartar build-up. Incorporating dental toys and treats can further complement your efforts, offering a fun and engaging way for your cat to clean their teeth. Vigilance for signs of dental issues is paramount, as early intervention can prevent minor problems from escalating into major ones.

Introducing your cat to daily brushing requires patience and persistence. Starting with short sessions and gradually increasing the duration as your cat becomes more comfortable can make a significant difference. Praise and treats can serve as positive reinforcement, creating a positive association with brushing.

CONCLUSION

Embarking on this journey of dental care with your cat is a testament to the depth of your love and commitment to their well-being. Through regular check-ups, a keen understanding of what to expect, and the selection of a skilled veterinary dentist, you're laying the foundation for a lifetime of health and happiness for your beloved pet. Furthermore, by incorporating dental care into your daily routine at home, you're ensuring that your cat's teeth remain clean, healthy, and strong. The path to dental wellness is a collaborative one, paved with dedication, knowledge, and love. Together, you and your cat can enjoy the countless benefits that come with optimal dental health, reinforcing the unbreakable bond you share.

"To care for a cat's teeth is to care for their whole being, nurturing not only their health but their joy for life."

CHAPTER 5

AT-HOME DENTAL CARE TECHNIQUES

WWW.WHISKERSANDPAWS.CO.NZ

INTRODUCTION

Hello, fellow cat lovers! You're embarking on a vital journey towards maintaining your cat's dental health, a crucial component of their overall well-being. Dental issues in cats can range from the minor inconvenience of halitosis (bad breath) to the more severe conditions like periodontal disease. However, the good news is that preventive measures, particularly at-home dental care, can significantly diminish these risks. This chapter aims to demystify the process of at-home dental care for cats, making it accessible and manageable for cat owners like you. We'll explore various methods to keep your cat's teeth clean and healthy, from brushing to dietary adjustments, and how to make dental care a positive experience for both you and your furry friend. The goal is to empower you with the knowledge and tools to prevent common dental issues, ensuring your cat enjoys a happy, healthy life with a bright smile.

METHODS OF AT-HOME DENTAL CARE

BRUSHING TEETH

Brushing your cat's teeth might seem like a daunting task initially, but it is undeniably one of the most effective ways to prevent plaque and tartar buildup, leading causes of dental disease in cats. The key to success lies in patience and gradual introduction. Start by familiarizing your cat with the toothbrush and toothpaste (opt for flavors designed to appeal to felines, like poultry or fish). Allow them to sniff and lick the toothpaste from your finger to build a positive association.

The actual brushing should be a slow and gentle process. Begin by brushing a couple of teeth and the gum line, gradually increasing the number of teeth cleaned over time. It's crucial to use a soft-brushed, cat-specific toothbrush and toothpaste, as human products can be harmful to cats. Consistency is key; aim for brushing sessions several times a week. While resistance from your cat is normal initially, most cats can learn to tolerate or even enjoy brushing with patience and positive reinforcement.

DENTAL TREATS AND DIETS

Dental treats and specialized diets offer an additional line of defense against dental problems. These products are formulated to help reduce plaque and tartar accumulation through mechanical action (chewing) and/or the inclusion of specific ingredients that promote oral health. When selecting dental treats, it's important to choose those endorsed by veterinary dental societies and to integrate them into your cat's diet in a balanced manner. Over-reliance on treats can lead to weight gain or nutritional imbalances, so they should complement, not replace, regular meals and brushing routines.

Despite their convenience, it's important to remember that dental treats and diets cannot wholly substitute the mechanical and comprehensive cleaning achieved through brushing. They are best used as part of a broader dental care strategy that includes regular brushing and professional dental check-ups.

DENTAL WIPES & GELS

Dental wipes and gels can serve as alternatives or supplements to brushing, especially for cats that vehemently resist toothbrushing. These products are designed to be rubbed along the teeth and gums, helping to remove some plaque and bacteria. It's essential to select items specifically formulated for cats to ensure safety and effectiveness. While these alternatives may offer a less thorough clean compared to brushing, they can still play a role in your cat's dental care routine by providing some level of plaque control and freshening breath.

However, it's critical to understand the limitations of wipes and gels. They should not be seen as direct substitutes for brushing but rather as part of a comprehensive approach to dental care that may also include dental treats, diets, and water additives.

WATER ADDITIVES

Water additives are a relatively simple and non-invasive way to support dental health. These products are added to your cat's drinking water and work to reduce plaque buildup and freshen breath. When choosing water additives, look for those that are vet-recommended and free of harmful ingredients. As with any dietary change or addition, it's important to introduce water additives gradually and monitor your cat's response, particularly their water intake, to ensure they remain well-hydrated.

While water additives can be an effective component of dental care, they should not be relied upon exclusively. The most effective dental care regimen includes a combination of brushing, the use of dental products like treats, wipes, or gels, and regular veterinary check-ups.

TIPS FOR MAKING THE PROCESS EASIER

Introducing your cat to dental care routines early in life can significantly ease the process. Kittens are generally more adaptable and can become accustomed to regular brushing and dental care activities as a normal part of their routine.

Creating a Positive Experience
The key to successful at-home dental care is making it a positive experience for your cat. Use praise, petting, and treats to reward your cat during and after dental care sessions. This positive reinforcement helps your cat associate dental care with enjoyable outcomes.

Routine and Consistency
Establishing a consistent routine is crucial for effective dental care. Regularity not only aids in preventing dental issues but also helps your cat become accustomed to the process, reducing resistance over time.

Patience and Persistence
It's normal for cats to resist dental care activities initially. However, with patience and persistent effort, most cats can learn to tolerate or even enjoy these sessions. If you encounter significant difficulties, consider seeking advice from a veterinarian or a professional pet trainer.

Seeking Professional Advice
Regular veterinary check-ups are an essential part of your cat's dental care routine. A professional can provide additional guidance, perform professional cleanings, and address any dental issues before they become more serious problems.

CONCLUSION

Embracing at-home dental care is a significant step towards ensuring your cat's long-term health and happiness. By integrating regular brushing, dietary management, and the use of dental hygiene products, you can significantly reduce the risk of dental diseases and contribute to your cat's overall well-being. Remember, while at-home care is crucial, it should complement regular veterinary check-ups for optimal dental health. Thank you for committing to your cat's dental health. With patience, persistence, and the right approach, you can make dental care a rewarding part of your life with your feline friend.

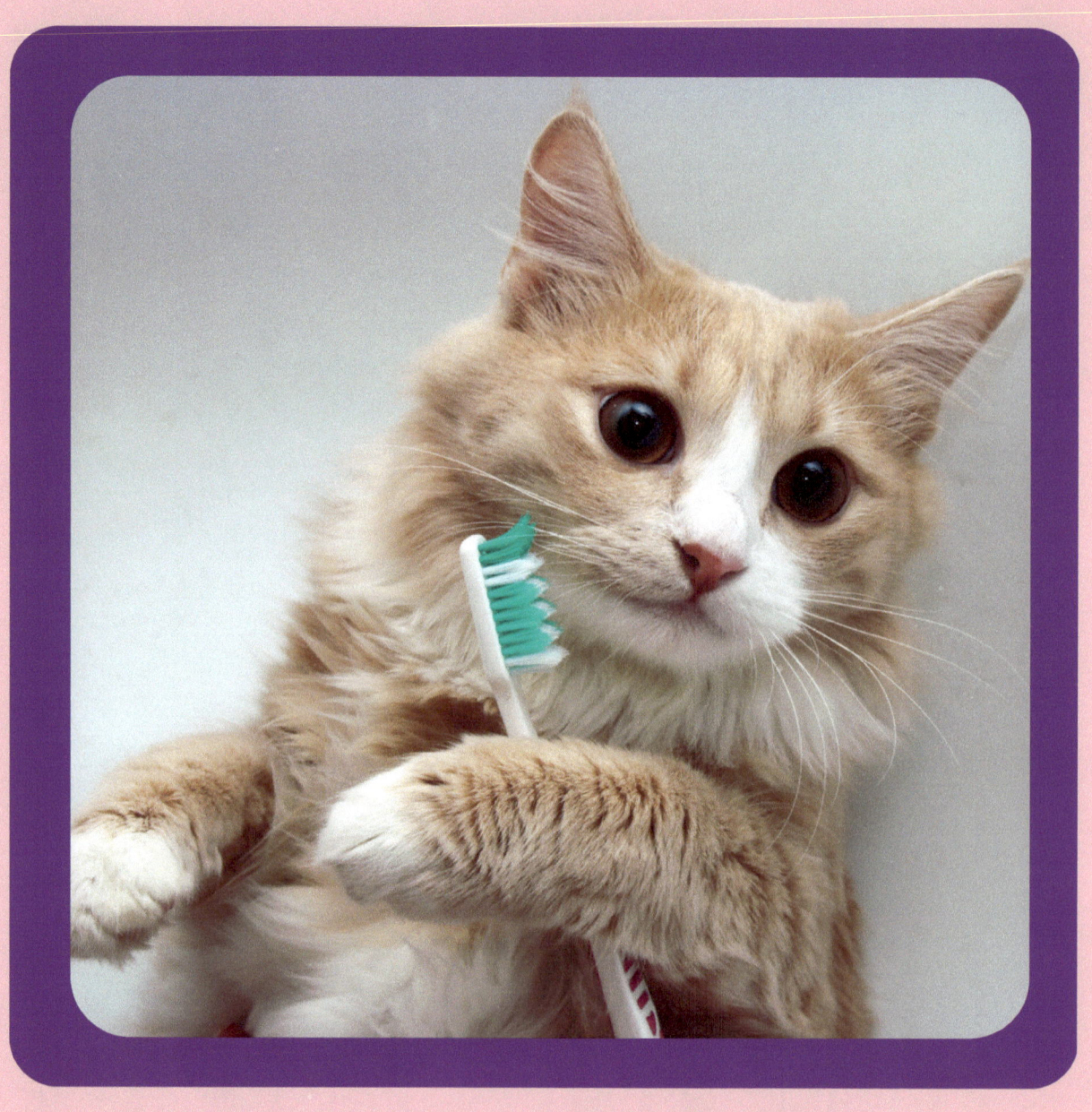

"A cat's fangs are as mysterious as their gaze—tiny, sharp symbols of strength, elegance, and the natural balance of play and protection."

CHAPTER 6

CHOOSING THE RIGHT DENTAL CARE PRODUCTS

WWW.WHISKERSANDPAWS.CO.NZ

INTRODUCTION

Hey there, fellow cat lover! Welcome to this crucial chapter on selecting the ideal dental care products for your furry friend. It's not just about battling bad breath (though, let's be honest, cuddles are more enjoyable when your cat's breath is fresh)-it's about their overall health and wellbeing. Neglecting dental care can lead to significant health problems, but fear not! We're here to guide you through the maze of products, ensuring you make informed decisions that will have your cat's teeth gleaming and their health in top shape. So, buckle up and prepare to dive deep into the world of feline dental care. Together, we'll explore how to keep your kitty's smile bright and healthy, ensuring they lead a happy, purr-filled life.

TYPES OF DENTAL CARE PRODUCTS FOR CATS

TOOTHBRUSHES FOR CATS

The journey to optimal dental health starts with the right toothbrush. Size and bristle softness are your compass here. A brush that's too big or with bristles too rough can turn toothbrushing into a struggle or, worse, harm your cat's delicate gums. Finger brushes and standard toothbrushes each have their merits. Finger brushes, fitting snugly over your fingertip, offer a gentle introduction to brushing for your cat. They're especially useful for pets that thrive on close contact. On the flip side, standard toothbrushes provide precision and reach, making them ideal for thorough cleanings. Whichever route you choose, introducing your cat to the concept of toothbrushing requires patience, love, and plenty of their favorite treats. Aim for a few brushing sessions a week to keep tartar and plaque at bay, and don't forget about brush maintenance-regular cleaning and timely replacement are key to effective dental care.

DENTAL TREATS AND DIETS

Imagine if snack time could also protect your cat's teeth. Enter dental treats and diets. These are not just tasty; they're designed to combat plaque and tartar buildup. The trick is to select treats with a seal of approval from reputable veterinary dental organizations. This ensures they meet specific oral health standards. However, moderation is key. Even the healthiest treats can contribute to weight gain if offered in excess. Keep an eye on your cat's intake to maintain their svelte figure. We'll dive into some of the most beloved brands later, giving you a head start on improving your cat's dental health deliciously.

WATER ADDITIVES

The secret ingredient in your cat's water bowl? A water additive designed for dental care. These ingenious products are a hassle-free way to bolster your cat's oral hygiene. By simply mixing an additive into their water, you can reduce plaque buildup and keep their breath fresh. It's an effortless addition to their daily routine, especially for the brush-averse feline. Choosing a product that's both tasteless and safe is crucial; your cat shouldn't even notice the difference. We'll explore some of the top vet-approved additives, ensuring your cat stays hydrated and healthy without any fuss.

DENTAL GELS, SPRAYS, AND WIPES

For the feline not fond of brushing, dental gels, sprays, and wipes offer a convenient alternative. These products are crafted to reduce plaque and freshen breath, no toothbrush required. The key is finding a format that suits both you and your cat. Some may prefer the simplicity of a wipe, while others might not mind a gel applied to their gums. Whichever option you choose, the goal is consistent use. Regular application is essential for these products to be effective. We'll guide you through the best picks, making it easier to incorporate dental care into your daily pet care routine.

CHOOSING BASED ON YOU CAT'SNEEDS

Cats are as individual as humans, each with their own preferences and health needs. This diversity extends to dental care. A thorough veterinary check-up can shed light on any specific issues your cat faces, guiding your product selection. Age, size, and temperament play significant roles in this choice. For example, a kitten might be more receptive to new experiences, including toothbrushing, while an older cat may prefer the less invasive approach of a dental gel. Also, consider your cat's health history. Cats with a predisposition to dental issues may benefit from specialized products. And remember, introducing any new item into your cat's routine should be a gradual process, filled with positive reinforcement.

RECOMMENDED BRANDS AND PRODUCTS

Now, let's talk specifics. When it comes to toothpaste, enzymatic options are a favorite. They work by breaking down plaque and tartar, often coming in flavors that cats can't resist. Dental treats should ideally carry the Veterinary Oral Health Council (VOHC) seal, indicating they've met rigorous dental health standards. For water additives, we'll highlight those that blend effectiveness with safety, providing an easy daily dental care boost. And let's not overlook innovative tools and toys designed to make dental care engaging for your cat. With the right products, you can turn dental hygiene into a bonding experience, ensuring your cat's teeth are clean and their health is protected.

CONCLUSION

Taking the leap into proactive dental care for your cat is commendable. It's a significant step toward preventing dental diseases and ensuring your cat enjoys a long, happy life by your side. Every small effort counts, from the daily water additive to the weekly toothbrushing session. Thank you for embarking on this journey with us. Your dedication to your cat's wellbeing is truly inspiring. Remember, consistency is the foundation of good dental health. Keep up the great work, and here's to countless joyful moments with your healthy, happy feline friend!

Expanding on the Importance of Dental Care

Understanding why dental care is so critical for your cat is the first step in committing to their oral health. Just like in humans, poor dental hygiene in cats can lead to a myriad of health issues, from minor problems like bad breath and tartar buildup to more severe conditions like periodontal disease, which can have systemic effects on the heart, liver, and kidneys. Regular dental care not only prevents these issues but can also improve your cat's quality of life, allowing them to eat comfortably and interact without pain or discomfort.

Introducing Toothbrushing Gradually

For many cats, toothbrushing is an unfamiliar sensation, which means patience and gradual introduction are key. Start by allowing your cat to sniff and explore the toothbrush and toothpaste, offering treats to create a positive association. You can then progress to gently touching their teeth and gums with your finger before finally using the toothbrush. Remember, the goal is to make this a positive experience, so never force the process and always praise your cat for their cooperation.

The Role of Professional Dental Care

While at-home dental care is essential, it's also important to incorporate professional dental check-ups and cleanings into your cat's healthcare routine. A veterinarian can provide a thorough examination of your cat's mouth, identifying any potential issues that may not be visible to the untrained eye. They can also perform professional cleanings, removing plaque and tartar buildup that can't be addressed with brushing alone. Regular veterinary visits ensure that any dental issues are caught and treated early, preventing more serious problems down the line.

Making Dental Care a Routine

Consistency is crucial when it comes to dental care. Establishing a routine makes it easier for both you and your cat to stick with it. Try to incorporate dental care activities into your daily routine, choosing times when your cat is most relaxed and receptive. Whether it's a quick brushing session or adding a dental treat to their evening meal, creating a consistent schedule helps cement these activities as part of your cat's normal routine, making them less likely to resist over time.

Engaging Your Cat in Dental Care

Finally, remember that dental care doesn't have to be a chore-for you or your cat. There are many ways to make these activities enjoyable and engaging. Playful interactions, such as treat-dispensing toys that promote chewing or flavored toothpastes that feel like a treat, can turn dental care into a fun part of your cat's day. By approaching dental care with a positive attitude and a bit of creativity, you can help ensure your cat's mouth remains healthy and pain-free, allowing them to enjoy a happier, more comfortable life.

"Hidden behind a soft purr and a gentle nuzzle are teeth that tell the story of a little lion, equal parts grace and strength."

CHAPTER 7

THE ROLE OF DIET IN DENTAL HEALTH

WWW.WHISKERSANDPAWS.CO.NZ

INTRODUCTION

Hey there! Welcome to a crucial part of our journey together, where we unlock the secrets to keeping your feline friend's teeth gleaming and healthy. Have you ever paused to think about the impact your cat's diet has on their dental health? Well, strap in because you're about to dive deep into how what your cat eats directly affects their smile. This chapter will guide you through the maze of dietary choices, shedding light on the best foods to fend off dental issues and keep your cat's pearly whites in top condition. Ready to become a savvy cat food shopper and a dental care pro? Let's leap into the wonderful world of cat nutrition and dental health.

IMPACT OF DIET ON DENTAL HEALTH

DRY VS. WET FOOD

The debate between dry and wet food is as old as time, or at least as long as commercial cat food has been around. Many believe that dry food, with its crunchy texture, acts like a toothbrush for cats, helping to scrape away plaque as they chew. This isn't entirely off the mark, but it's not the full picture either. On the flip side, wet food provides essential hydration and may be easier on the teeth of older cats or those with dental issues, though it lacks the mechanical cleaning action dry food offers. So, the question remains: Which is better for your cat's dental health? The answer isn't straightforward, as both types of food have their merits and drawbacks in terms of dental hygiene. We'll explore how to strike the perfect balance, ensuring your cat enjoys the benefits of both while keeping their teeth and gums healthy.

Special Dental Diets

Imagine a diet meticulously crafted to safeguard your cat's dental health, where every bite is designed to clean their teeth. Special dental diets do precisely that, offering a unique solution to the battle against plaque and tartar buildup. These diets are engineered to be tougher and more challenging to chew, providing a natural abrasive action that helps keep the teeth clean. But how effective are they, really? We'll delve into the mechanics of these diets, examining their benefits and limitations, and whether they could be the secret weapon in your arsenal for maintaining your cat's dental health.

The Role of Nutrition

Nutrition plays a stealthy but significant role in dental health, with certain vitamins and minerals acting as the guardians of your cat's gums and teeth. A diet lacking in these essential nutrients can lead to weak teeth and unhealthy gums, predisposing your furry companion to a host of dental problems. But which nutrients should you be on the lookout for? We're going to break down the nutritional components critical for strong dental health, from calcium and phosphorus to vitamins A and D, and how they work together to fortify your cat's teeth against disease.

Food Ingredients to Avoid

Not all ingredients are created equal, especially when it comes to your cat's dental health. Some culprits, like sugary foods, can do more harm than good, promoting bacterial growth and leading to tooth decay and gum disease. Identifying these harmful ingredients is key to making informed dietary choices for your cat. We'll guide you through the process of scrutinizing food labels, helping you to avoid common pitfalls and select foods that support rather than undermine your cat's dental health.

Understanding Food Labels

Navigating the world of cat food labels can feel like deciphering an ancient code. With a maze of ingredients, nutritional information, and marketing claims, how do you determine which foods are genuinely good for your cat's dental health? Fear not, for we're here to demystify the process, providing you with the knowledge to cut through the jargon and make sense of what's really in your cat's food. By understanding what to look for and what to avoid, you'll be equipped to make choices that not only please your cat's palate but also contribute to their dental well-being.

CHOOSING THE RIGHT FOOD

VOHC Seal of Acceptance

In your quest for the perfect dental diet for your cat, you may come across products boasting the Veterinary Oral Health Council (VOHC) Seal of Acceptance. This seal is more than just a fancy sticker; it's a mark of quality, indicating that the product meets stringent criteria for reducing plaque and tartar buildup. But what does it really mean for your cat's dental health, and how should it influence your buying decisions? We'll explore the significance of the VOHC seal, which products have earned this endorsement, and how they can fit into your overall strategy for keeping your cat's teeth clean and healthy.

Age and Health Considerations

Cats, like people, have varying nutritional needs throughout their lives, influenced by their age, health status, and unique physiological requirements. These factors can significantly impact their dental health and should guide your decisions when selecting their food. For instance, kittens have different dietary needs compared to senior cats, who may struggle with dental issues and require softer foods. Similarly, cats with specific health conditions might benefit from tailored diets designed to support their dental and overall health. We'll walk you through the process of choosing the right food for your cat at every stage of their life, ensuring their diet promotes dental health and supports their well-being.

Consulting with a Veterinarian

Navigating the complexities of cat nutrition and dental health can be daunting, but you don't have to do it alone. Your veterinarian is a valuable resource, offering expert advice tailored to your cat's individual needs. Whether you're considering a special dental diet or simply looking to optimize your cat's nutritional intake, consulting with your vet can provide the insights you need to make informed decisions. We'll discuss how to make the most of your vet visits, the questions to ask, and how professional guidance can help you select the best diet for your cat's dental and overall health.

Trial and Error in Diet Selection

Finding the perfect diet for your cat is often a process of trial and error. Cats are notorious for their finicky eating habits, and what works for one may not appeal to another. Moreover, the impact of a particular diet on dental health can vary from cat to cat. We'll share strategies for introducing new foods, monitoring your cat's response, and adjusting their diet as needed to find the optimal balance between taste and dental health benefits.

Balancing Diet and Dental Health

Achieving the ideal balance between a diet your cat loves and one that supports their dental health is the ultimate goal. This delicate balancing act requires understanding your cat's preferences, nutritional needs, and the role of diet in preventing dental issues. We'll explore practical ways to integrate dental health considerations into your cat's diet without compromising on the enjoyment and satisfaction they derive from their meals.

Choosing Dental Chews

Dental chews offer a convenient and enjoyable way to supplement your cat's dental care regimen, helping to clean teeth and freshen breath. But with so many options on the market, how do you choose the right ones? We'll examine the different types of dental chews available, their benefits and limitations, and what to look for when selecting the best dental chews for your cat.

Healthy Snack Options

Believe it or not, certain fruits and vegetables can make excellent dental health snacks for your cat. While not all cats will take to these options, those that do can benefit from the additional nutrients and the natural abrasive action of chewing on these healthy treats.

Homemade Dental Treats

If you're feeling adventurous, making your own dental treats can be a fun and rewarding way to care for your cat's teeth. Homemade treats allow you to control the ingredients, ensuring they're healthy and beneficial for your cat's dental health. We'll share simple, vet-approved recipes for creating tasty dental treats at home, allowing you to add a personal touch to your cat's dental care.

Frequency and Quantity of Treats

While treats can be a valuable tool in promoting dental health, moderation is key. Overindulging your cat with treats, no matter how healthy, can lead to weight gain and other health issues. We'll provide guidelines on the appropriate frequency and quantity of dental health snacks and treats, helping you strike the right balance between rewarding your cat and maintaining their oral health.

CONCLUSION

Congratulations on taking this comprehensive journey through the role of diet in your cat's dental health. By now, you're armed with the knowledge and tools to make informed dietary choices that will not only delight your cat but also help keep their teeth strong and healthy. Your commitment to your cat's dental care is a testament to the deep bond you share, and your efforts will undoubtedly lead to a happier, healthier life together. Remember, the path to optimal dental health is a collaborative one, involving you, your cat, and your veterinarian. Keep up the fantastic work, and here's to many more years of joyful purrs and healthy smiles!

"In every whiskered grin and gentle nip lies a cat's wild spirit. Their teeth are tiny tools, perfected by nature for play, precision, and power."

CHAPTER 8

UNDERSTANDING CAT DENTAL PROCEDURES

WWW.WHISKERSANDPAWS.CO.NZ

INTRODUCTION

Welcome to the enlightening journey of understanding cat dental procedures. If you've found your way here, it's clear you have a deep affection for your furry companions and wish for them to lead a joyful, healthy life. A significant, yet often overlooked, aspect of ensuring this is by paying close attention to their dental health. Dental care for cats is not just about maintaining a sparkling smile; it's about preventing a host of potential health issues that can affect their overall well-being. So, buckle up as we delve into the intricacies of cat dental care, providing you with the knowledge to help your cat through these procedures and ensuring a swift recovery. By the end of this exploration, you'll be more than equipped to handle your cat's dental needs with confidence.

Understanding the various dental procedures your cat may undergo is crucial for any cat owner. Dental issues in cats are not rare; in fact, they're quite common and can lead to serious health complications if left untreated. The journey begins with recognizing the importance of dental check-ups, the cornerstone of preventive dental care. Regular visits to the vet can catch issues early, before they escalate into larger problems requiring more complex procedures such as tooth extractions or even surgery.

DENTAL CHECK UP

The annual dental check-up is an essential part of your cat's health routine. Think of it as a yearly wellness exam, focusing on their oral health. During these check-ups, the veterinarian will thoroughly examine your cat's mouth, checking for any signs of gum disease, tooth resorption, or other dental conditions. They might also discuss your current dental care routine at home and suggest improvements or changes, like introducing specific dental health diets or toys. Regular check-ups are your first line of defense against dental diseases, aiming to catch and address problems early.

PROFESSIONAL DENTAL CLEAN

Professional dental cleanings go beyond what you can do with a toothbrush at home. This procedure, typically done under anesthesia, allows the vet to clean your cat's teeth thoroughly, removing plaque and tartar buildup that can lead to periodontal disease. Anesthesia is necessary for this procedure, not just for the safety of the veterinary staff but also to ensure a thorough cleaning without causing stress or pain to your cat. Post-cleaning, it's normal for cats to experience some grogginess, but this usually wears off within a few hours. The benefits of professional cleanings are immense, contributing significantly to your cat's oral and overall health.

TOOTH EXTRACTIONS

At times, despite our best efforts, a tooth may need to be removed. Tooth extractions are common procedures, often necessary due to severe decay, injury, or other dental issues. The thought of your cat undergoing an extraction can be worrying, but it's a procedure that can vastly improve their quality of life. Recovery from a tooth extraction involves plenty of rest, a soft food diet, and close monitoring for any signs of pain or infection. With your loving care, your cat will soon be back to their usual self, free from the discomfort they were experiencing.

DENTAL X-RAYS

Dental X-rays are invaluable tools in veterinary dental care, offering a glimpse below the gumline and revealing problems invisible to the naked eye. These X-rays are crucial for diagnosing underlying issues and planning for procedures like tooth extractions or addressing periodontal disease. The process is quick, painless, and provides essential information for maintaining your cat's dental health.

WHAT TO EXPECT DURING AND AFTER DENTAL PROCEDURES

Understanding what happens during and after your cat's dental procedures can help alleviate any anxiety you might have. Anesthesia plays a vital role in ensuring these procedures are stress-free and painless for your cat. While the thought of anesthesia may be daunting, veterinary professionals are well-equipped to monitor and maintain your cat's safety throughout the procedure. Post-operative care is equally important, with your vet providing detailed instructions on managing your cat's recovery. This might include administering pain relief, dietary adjustments, and tips on keeping your cat comfortable as they heal.

TIPS FOR POST-PROCEDURE CARE

The success of your cat's recovery often hinges on the post-procedure care they receive. Following your veterinarian's instructions is paramount, as is creating a tranquil environment for your cat to recuperate. Monitoring your cat closely in the days following a procedure is crucial for spotting any signs of distress or complications early. Soft foods can help ease the transition back to eating, especially after tooth extractions, and minimizing vigorous play can prevent unnecessary strain on your recovering cat. Above all, your patience, understanding, and affection will provide immense comfort to your cat, supporting them through their recovery.

As we wrap up this journey into the world of cat dental procedures, it's clear that dental health is an integral component of your cat's overall well-being. From preventive measures like regular check-ups and cleanings to more involved procedures such as tooth extractions and the use of dental X-rays, each aspect plays a vital role in ensuring your cat leads a happy, healthy life. By embracing the information provided and applying it to your cat's dental care routine, you're taking significant steps toward safeguarding their health and happiness. Remember, your efforts today lay the foundation for a future filled with joyous purrs, cozy cuddles, and, most importantly, a healthy, vibrant cat.

Now, let's dive a bit deeper into some of the nuances and often overlooked aspects of cat dental care that can make a big difference in how you approach these procedures.

THE EMOTIONAL ASPECT OF DENTAL PROCEDURES

It's not uncommon for cat owners to feel a mix of anxiety and concern when their beloved pet needs to undergo dental procedures. Recognizing and addressing these feelings is an important part of preparing for your cat's dental care. Remember, your calm and positive demeanor can influence your cat's emotional state before and after the procedure, making the experience less stressful for both of you.

Choosing the Right Veterinary Clinic

Selecting a veterinary clinic that has a good reputation for dental care and is equipped with the necessary tools and expertise is crucial. Don't hesitate to ask your vet about their experience with cat dental procedures, the types of anesthesia and monitoring equipment they use, and their protocols for managing pain and recovery. This information can provide you with peace of mind, knowing that your cat is in capable hands.

Nutrition and Dental Health

Diet plays a significant role in your cat's dental health. Discuss with your vet the best dietary options for supporting your cat's oral health, including foods that promote dental hygiene. Some diets are specifically formulated to reduce plaque and tartar buildup, and your veterinarian can recommend products that suit your cat's specific needs and preferences.

The Role of Dental Toys and Treats

Incorporating dental toys and treats into your cat's routine can be a fun and effective way to support their dental health. These products are designed to help reduce plaque and tartar buildup through the natural action of chewing. Ask your veterinarian for recommendations on safe and effective dental toys and treats that your cat will love.

Regular Home Dental Care

In addition to professional care, establishing a regular dental care routine at home is vital. Brushing your cat's teeth may seem daunting at first, but with patience and practice, it can become a bonding experience for you and your cat. Start slowly, using a toothbrush and toothpaste specifically designed for cats, and gradually increase the frequency of brushing as your cat becomes more accustomed to it.

The Importance of Early Detection

One of the key messages in understanding cat dental procedures is the importance of early detection in preventing more serious health issues. Regular dental check-ups and being vigilant about changes in your cat's oral health can lead to early intervention, significantly improving the outcome of dental procedures and your cat's overall health.

CONCLUSION

Taking an active role in your cat's dental care through regular check-ups, professional cleanings, and a solid at-home care routine can lead to a lifetime of healthy smiles. Your dedication to understanding and managing your cat's dental health is a testament to the deep bond and love you share. With the knowledge and tips provided in this chapter, you're well on your way to ensuring your furry friend enjoys a happy, healthy life with a clean, bright smile.

"A cat's teeth are small but mighty, a reminder of the predator within the pet, ready for adventure in every nibble and play-bite."

CHAPTER 9

PREVENTING DENTAL PROBLEMS

WWW.WHISKERSANDPAWS.CO.NZ

INTRODUCTION

Hey there, fellow cat-parent! Welcome to this crucial part of our journey together. Caring for your cat goes beyond providing love, shelter, and nutrition; it extends into ensuring they maintain a sparkling, healthy set of teeth. Have you ever noticed your cat turning their nose up at their food, or perhaps their breath could give their litter box a run for its money in terms of pungency? These could be telltale signs of dental problems lurking in their mouth. But fear not! You're about to step into a proactive role, armed with knowledge and tools to safeguard those pearly whites. Cats can encounter a spectrum of dental issues, ranging from the mild inconvenience of bad breath to more severe conditions like periodontal disease, which can drastically impact not just their mood but their overall health. This is why taking preventative measures is not just beneficial; it's crucial for your cat's well-being. The good news? You're perfectly capable of being the superhero in your cat's dental health story. This chapter will guide you through effective strategies, offering tips and how-tos designed to fend off dental woes. So let's embark on this path to ensuring our feline friends lead a happy, healthy life, free from dental distress.

UNDERSTANDING DENTAL HEALTH

Understanding Dental Health

Before we dive deeper into prevention, let's take a moment to understand why dental health is so vital for our furry companions. Just like in humans, poor dental health in cats can lead to a myriad of problems. It's not just about bad breath; dental issues can lead to pain, making eating difficult, and can even cause infections that may spread to other parts of the body, including vital organs. Ensuring your cat's teeth and gums are healthy is about more than just oral care; it's about ensuring their overall health and longevity.

Regular Dental Check-Ups

Venturing into the realm of regular dental check-ups marks the first step in our preventative care journey. Yes, the prospect of convincing your cat that the carrier is not a monster might seem daunting. However, these visits are the cornerstone of preemptive dental care. Think of your veterinarian as the Gandalf of cat dental health, armed with wisdom and tools to guide you through the shadowy realms of dental disease. During these check-ups, your vet becomes a detective of sorts, exploring the nooks and crannies of your cat's mouth for signs of dental distress. They'll be on the lookout for plaque build-up, loose teeth, and might even suggest dental x-rays to peer into the hidden recesses below the gumline. It's essentially a spa day for your cat's mouth, albeit without the soothing ambiance of cucumber eye patches.

CREATING A POSITIVE VET VISIT EXPERIENCE

One of the biggest challenges cat owners face is the stress associated with vet visits. To make this experience more positive for your cat, start by making the carrier a familiar place. Leave it open in a space your cat frequents, with a comfortable blanket inside. Occasionally place treats or toys inside to encourage curiosity and positive associations. On the day of the visit, maintain a calm demeanor, as cats can pick up on our anxieties, which can, in turn, heighten their own.

Teaching Teeth Brushing Techniques

Brushing your cat's teeth might sound like a task best left to the bravest of souls, but it's a pivotal aspect of dental care. You'll need two essential tools: a cat-specific toothbrush and pet-safe toothpaste (chicken flavor might just be the ticket). Begin with patience, introducing your cat to the toothbrush and toothpaste separately, allowing them to become familiar with these new objects without any pressure. When it comes to the actual brushing, use gentle, circular motions and aim to cover all their teeth. Remember, the experience should be as positive as possible, so conclude each session with plenty of praise or a treat. If your cat decides they're not a fan of this new activity, don't despair. Consistency and patience are your allies here. While daily brushing is the gold standard, managing a few times a week is still a win in the battle against plaque and tartar.

BUILDING UP TO BRUSHING

If your cat is initially resistant to brushing, don't force the issue. Instead, gradually build up their tolerance. Start by using your finger (covered with a clean, soft cloth) to gently rub their gums and teeth. Once they become accustomed to this sensation, introduce the toothbrush without toothpaste, allowing them to sniff and lick it. Gradually, as they become more comfortable, you can start adding toothpaste and moving on to brushing. Celebrate small victories; even getting a few teeth brushed at a time is progress.

Dental Diets and Treats

What your cat eats plays a significant role in their dental health. This is where dental diets and treats enter the stage, acting as your tasty allies in the fight against dental issues. These aren't just any treats or kibble; they're designed to do double duty by satisfying your cat's hunger while also cleaning their teeth with every chew. When shopping for these dental champions, keep an eye out for products that boast the Veterinary Oral Health Council (VOHC) seal of approval. This ensures that you're choosing items proven to have a positive effect on dental health. However, it's crucial to remember that while these diets and treats are beneficial, they cannot replace the need for regular brushing or veterinary check-ups.

Choosing the Right Dental Diets and Treats

Not all dental diets and treats are created equal. When selecting these products, look beyond the marketing. Research the ingredients, and understand what benefits they offer. Products that are hard and require chewing can be more effective in scrubbing away plaque than softer items. Also, consider your cat's dietary needs and preferences. If your cat has specific health issues or is picky about their food, you may need to try a few different brands before finding the right fit.

Incorporating Dental Toys

Toys are typically seen as instruments of fun, but they can also play a vital role in your cat's dental care regimen. Dental toys, specifically designed to promote chewing, can help manage plaque build-up in a fun and engaging way. When selecting these toys, look for ones made from safe, durable materials to ensure they can withstand your cat's enthusiastic play. Introducing these toys during playtime not only strengthens your bond with your cat but also sneaks in some extra dental care. Keep a watchful eye on how your cat interacts with their toys, and be ready to replace any that show signs of wear and tear. The goal is to keep playtime both fun and beneficial for dental health.

The Importance of Variety in Dental Toys

Just like humans, cats can become bored with the same old toys. To keep their interest piqued, rotate their dental toys regularly. This not only keeps them engaged but also exposes their teeth to different textures and cleaning mechanisms. Some dental toys incorporate bristles or mesh materials that mimic the action of brushing, while others are designed to massage the gums. Offering a variety of these toys can make dental care an exciting part of your cat's day.

Using Water Additives

Think of water additives as the secret ingredient in your cat's water bowl, silently working to bolster their dental health. These additives aim to reduce plaque and freshen breath, offering a simple yet effective way to enhance your cat's dental care routine. When selecting a water additive, it's important to choose one that's tasteless and safe for pets to ensure your cat's drinking habits remain unaffected. Introducing the additive gradually can help ensure acceptance, maintaining the vital hydration every cat needs.

The Role of Water Additives in Dental Health

Water additives are an excellent supplementary tool in your cat's dental care arsenal. They work by altering the chemistry of your cat's saliva, reducing the ability of plaque to stick to their teeth. Some additives also contain ingredients that help to break down existing plaque and tartar.

Concluding with Long-term Strategies for Prevention

Congratulations are in order; you've navigated through the myriad of tips and strategies designed to prevent dental problems in your cat. Though establishing a comprehensive dental care routine may seem daunting at first glance, your dedication will significantly impact your cat's health and happiness. Consistency is key in this endeavor; regular vet visits, diligent home care, and a commitment to learning and adapting your approach will ensure your cat enjoys a life free from dental distress. Your efforts will not only enhance your cat's quality of life but also fortify the bond you share. Here's to many more years of joy, companionship, and clean teeth!

"A cat's teeth are nature's perfect blend of beauty and function—delicate tools for grooming, play, and the occasional fierce display."

CHAPTER 10

THE IMPACT OF DENTAL HEALTH ON OVERALL WELLNESS

WWW.WHISKERSANDPAWS.CO.NZ

INTRODUCTION

Hey there, fellow cat enthusiast! Welcome to a super important chapter of our journey together-where we're diving deep into the world of cat dental health. Now, I know what you might be thinking: "Dental health? For my cat? Why should that be a big deal?" Well, let me tell you, it's a *huge* deal, and it's something that's often overlooked in the grand scheme of pet care. This chapter isn't just about teeth; it's about understanding how those pearly whites (or not-so-pearly ones) can actually tell us a lot about our furry friend's overall health and happiness. Stick with me, and by the end of this chapter, you'll be a pro at spotting dental issues and knowing just what to do to keep your cat's smile bright and healthy. So, let's jump right in!

CONNECTION BETWEEN DENTAL HEALTH AND OVERALL WELLNESS

Think of your cat's mouth as a window to their health. Just like in humans, a bunch of health issues can start in the mouth. Did you know that problems in the mouth can actually affect other parts of the body? Yep, it's true! When cats have dental issues, the bacteria from their mouth can get into their bloodstream and travel around, potentially causing trouble in organs like the heart, liver, and kidneys. That's why keeping those teeth clean isn't just about avoiding bad breath-it's about keeping your whole cat healthy.

But it's not just the big scares that should have us paying attention. Dental health affects more mundane yet crucial aspects of our cats' lives, like their ability to eat comfortably and their overall mood. A cat with a toothache is not a happy cat, and this discomfort can lead to more serious health issues, like malnutrition and dehydration, if they're avoiding food and water because it hurts to eat.

Ignoring your cat's dental health can lead to some pretty gnarly consequences. It starts with a bit of bad breath, but it can quickly turn into something much more serious, like tooth resorption (which is as painful as it sounds), or even systemic diseases that affect your cat's major organs. Early signs of dental problems can be subtle-maybe your cat isn't eating as much, or they're drooling more than usual. Catching these signs early means you can prevent a whole cascade of health issues down the line.

Plus, ignoring these early signs can lead not only to more complicated health issues but also to higher medical bills down the road. Early intervention is key to keeping both your cat healthy and your wallet happy. Regular dental check-ups can catch issues before they become serious, saving you both stress and money.

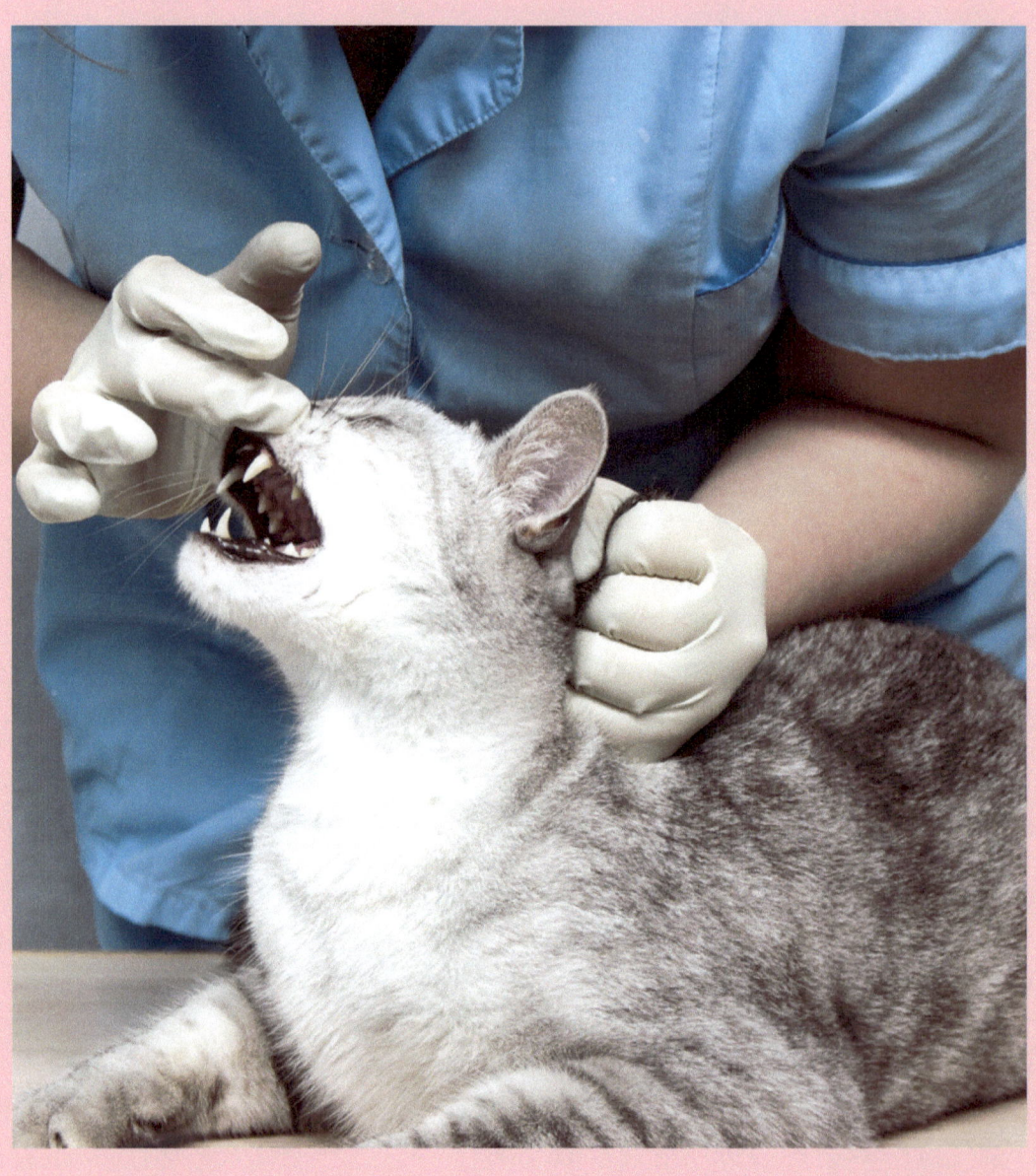

CONNECTION BETWEEN DENTAL HEALTH AND OVERALL WELLNESS

What your cat eats plays a big role in their dental health. Some foods are better than others for keeping those chompers in good shape. Dental health chews and treats can help, and so can certain types of food designed to reduce plaque and tartar build-up. But it's not just about dental health-good nutrition supports your cat's overall well-being, too. Making sure your cat has a balanced diet is a key part of keeping those teeth (and the rest of them) healthy.

This is because the right nutrients can strengthen your cat's teeth and gums from the inside out. Vitamins and minerals play a critical role in dental health, just as they do in overall health. For instance, calcium and phosphorus support strong teeth, while vitamin C supports gum health. Understanding the nutritional needs of your cat can help you choose the best diet for their dental and overall health.

It's also worth noting that not all cat foods are created equal when it comes to dental health. Some are specially formulated to help clean teeth as your cat eats. These can be a great addition to your cat's diet, but they should complement-not replace-regular dental care routines.

DAILY DENTAL CARE PRACTICES

Brushing your cat's teeth might sound like a daunting task, but it's an essential part of their care routine. Don't worry, we'll go step by step to make it as easy as possible. Consistency is key; making dental care a regular part of your cat's routine can prevent a lot of problems down the road. And there are plenty of products out there to help, from toothbrushes designed for cats to dental rinses. Just remember, not all products are created equal, so let's make sure you know what to look for.

Getting started with brushing can be a challenge, especially if your cat isn't used to it. It's best to start slow, introducing your cat to the toothbrush and letting them get used to the sensation. There are also finger brushes available, which might be less intimidating for your feline friend at first.

Creating a routine is just as important for dental care as it is for other aspects of your cat's life. Try to brush their teeth at the same time each day, so they come to expect it as part of their daily activities. This can help reduce stress for both of you and make the process smoother.

PROFESSIONAL DENTAL CARE: WHAT TO EXPECT

Even with the best at-home care, your cat will still need professional check-ups and cleanings. These visits are super important for catching any issues early and keeping your cat's mouth in tip-top shape. We'll talk about what to expect during these visits, how to prepare your cat, and what you can do afterward to keep their teeth as healthy as possible.

The first visit might be a bit overwhelming for your cat, so it's important to prepare them as much as possible. This can include getting them used to being in their carrier and taking short trips in the car. Your vet can also provide advice on how to make the visit less stressful for your cat.

During the check-up, your vet will examine your cat's teeth and gums, looking for any signs of disease or discomfort. They may also recommend a professional cleaning, which is done under anesthesia. While the thought of anesthesia might be scary, it's necessary to ensure a thorough cleaning and to keep your cat safe during the procedure.

INNOVATIONS IN FELINE DENTAL HEALTH

The world of feline dental care is always advancing, and there are some pretty cool innovations out there to help keep your cat's teeth healthy. From new types of dental treats to cutting-edge cleaning technologies, we'll explore what's new and what might be right for your cat.

One exciting innovation is in the area of dental health products. There are now water additives and gels that can help reduce plaque and tartar build-up, making daily care even easier. These products can be a great addition to your routine, especially if your cat isn't a fan of brushing.

Another area of innovation is in professional dental care. Laser therapy, for example, is becoming more common for treating gum disease in cats. This minimally invasive option can reduce pain and recovery time, making dental procedures easier on your feline friend.

Give yourself a pat on the back-you've just taken a huge step toward keeping your cat healthy and happy! By understanding the crucial connection between dental health and overall wellness, you're now equipped to tackle any dental issues head-on. Remember, your efforts make a world of difference in your cat's life, and there's nothing more rewarding than that. So, thank you for joining me on this journey, and here's to many happy, healthy years with your purrfect companion!

"In every tooth, a cat holds a legacy of wildness, softened by companionship but never fully tamed."

CHAPTER 11

CONCLUSION: CARING FOR YOUR CAT'S TEETH: A LIFELONG COMMITMENT

WWW.WHISKERSANDPAWS.CO.NZ

CONCLUSION

A conclusion that begins by recapping the importance of feline dental care, then reaffirms the owner's role in maintaining their cat's dental health, and ends with a call to action for lifelong care.

Introduction

Hey there, fellow cat lovers! Welcome aboard a crucial journey that promises to transform you into a hero in the eyes of your beloved feline companion. This adventure is all about mastering the art of cat dental care, a superpower that ensures your kitty remains in the pink of health, exuding happiness and vibrancy. If you've ever pondered the necessity of brushing your cat's teeth, rest assured, you're not alone in this thought. However, it's important to understand that, similar to humans, cats face their share of dental dilemmas. Plaque and gum disease are not just minor inconveniences; left unattended, they can escalate into significant health concerns.

Dental care for cats transcends mere breath freshening. It's about averting discomfort and diseases that could dampen your cat's quality of life. As a committed cat owner, your role is pivotal. While treats and cuddles are appreciated, delving into the essence of dental care is crucial. Fear not, the journey is far from daunting. On the contrary, it's filled with rewarding milestones, each one enhancing your cat's health and happiness.

Let's embark on this enlightening path, armed with knowledge and determination, to ensure our feline friends enjoy optimal dental health. Are you ready to dive in? Let's begin this fulfilling endeavor together.

Understanding Your Cat's Dental Needs

Imagine taking a mini-tour inside a cat's mouth. Picture the sharp teeth designed for tearing food, highlighting the importance of maintaining these dental tools in pristine condition. Cats are prone to dental diseases, much like their human counterparts, with periodontal disease leading the charge. This ailment begins its journey with plaque accumulation and can advance to inflamed, bleeding gums, resulting in tooth loss if not addressed timely.

The indicators of dental distress in cats are not always overt. Bad breath, reluctance or difficulty in eating, and any form of discomfort around the mouth area signal underlying dental issues. Neglecting these signs can have far-reaching consequences, including infections that might affect other bodily functions. The silver lining? These scenarios are preventable through proactive dental care, ensuring your cat's mouth remains a fortress against diseases.

Daily Dental Care Routines

Venturing into the world of feline dental care, the first order of business is selecting appropriate tools. Cat-specific toothbrushes and toothpaste are essential; human dental care products are off-limits due to potential harm to your pet. The thought of brushing your cat's teeth might evoke images of a mini-battle, but fear not. With patience and a gentle approach, this activity can morph into a bonding experience.

Begin this ritual with baby steps, gradually acclimatizing your cat to the process. Remember, consistency is the backbone of dental care success. Incorporating this practice into your daily routine wards off dental diseases and keeps your cat's oral health in check.

Professional Dental Care

Despite diligent home care, your cat requires periodic professional dental check-ups. These veterinary visits are instrumental in detecting potential issues early on, ensuring your cat's dental health remains on the right track. Professional cleanings, although potentially costly, are an investment in your cat's overall well-being. Exploring pet insurance options that cover dental procedures can mitigate these expenses, ensuring your furry friend receives the necessary care without financial strain.

Diet and Dental Health

The correlation between diet and dental health cannot be overstated. Dry food serves a dual purpose: nourishing your cat and aiding in plaque removal. Additionally, the market offers diets formulated specifically for dental health, alongside treats that contribute positively to this aspect. However, it's crucial to balance these treats within the framework of a comprehensive diet, ensuring your cat's nutritional needs are met comprehensively.

Common Challenges and Solutions

Cats, with their diverse personalities and health profiles, present unique challenges in dental care. Senior cats, for instance, might grapple with tooth loss or require specific dietary adjustments. Furthermore, not all cats are amenable to having their teeth brushed, but don't let this deter you. Patience, perseverance, and a dollop of love are key ingredients in overcoming these hurdles.

By engaging in this chapter, you've taken a monumental step towards safeguarding your cat's dental health. This journey is marked by commitment, a prerequisite for fostering a happy, healthy cat. Your dedication is the cornerstone of your cat's well-being, underscoring the importance of initiating and maintaining proper dental care practices. It's a testament to the fact that it's never too late to start, and every effort, no matter how small, paves the way toward a brighter, healthier future for your cat.

The path to optimal feline dental health is a collective journey, enriched by your unwavering commitment and the invaluable insights shared in this guide. As we conclude, take a moment to acknowledge the strides you've made in understanding and implementing the facets of cat dental care. Your efforts resonate deeply, enhancing the bond between you and your cat, and setting the stage for a lifetime of health and happiness.

In the spirit of continuous care and dedication, let's pledge to keep the momentum going. Embrace each day as an opportunity to enrich your cat's life, ensuring that their smiles-though hidden beneath whiskers-remain as healthy and vibrant as ever. Together, let's champion the cause of feline dental health, making every day a milestone in our quest for their well-being.

""A cat's purr soothes, but their teeth remind us of their wild heart—an exquisite balance of softness and strength."

Dedicated to my mother-

Wendy Jean Moffatt

She never got to share our dream of running the cat resort together due to her Alzheimers Disease.
RIP 13/3/2024